Never Buy a Raccoon at a Gas Station

Life Lessons for Children of All Ages

By Beth Detjens

Copyright © 2019 Beth Detjens

ISBN: 9780578443270

ISBN-13: 978 9780578443270

First printing January 2019

Dedication

This book is dedicated to my sweet Mom, who survived our family's adventures with grace and patience that remains unrivaled to this day.

Contents

Preface

In the interest of full disclosure, I have to tell you a few things about this book.

Every story you'll read here actually happened — unbelievably, often unfortunately — it all happened. Thanks to my middle-aged memory, I had to fill in a few details with my best guess, but about 90% of what you'll read here actually happened exactly as it's described. The rest definitely fits the spirit, if not the actual facts, of the story.

The lessons that accompany these stories aren't particularly deep, but these simple truths learned from our adventures with Bandit have served our family well.

Despite how fun my childhood adventures with animals were, I in no way condone or recommend removing wildlife from their natural habitat unless it is within the legal and humane confines of organized animal rescue operations. Leading with our hearts instead of our heads often could have ended in disaster.

That brings me to my final disclaimer, and possibly a bit of a spoiler. Despite coming perilously close at times, we all survived this crazy but fun season of our lives. It was touch-and-go at times, but we made it. And what we learned about ourselves and nature has served us in incalculable ways.

I hope you enjoy reading these stories as much as my family enjoyed living them. You might shake your head and wonder how and why our family had so many uncommon animals. The short answer — my eccentric dad and my incredibly gracious mom.

Acknowledgments

And now for the most important part — my heartfelt gratitude for an amazing and wonderful family. I would like to thank my husband and kids for their constant support, which made this book possible. I love you more than words can say. And no, we can not have a pet raccoon.

To my original family, whom you are about to meet, thank you for the most wonderful childhood.

Thank you, first and foremost to my mom, who is *the* most loving, patient and wise person I know. You went along with our crazy ideas, but you made sure we all learned as much as possible from them. I'm glad you put your foot down when reason forsook everyone else in the family — like that time you vetoed the baby bear cub that I begged for. Thank you.

Thank you to my beautiful and loving sister, who was so often the voice of reason that kept us grounded. I'm really sorry that our skunk sprayed when I tricked you into looking in that bucket. And I'm sorry for all the boyfriends our raccoon Bandit scared away — especially when I put him up to it. There is no one else I would have chosen to share our childhood with. You are my heart, and I love you so.

Last, but most definitely not least, thank you, Dad, for your fearless dedication to animal welfare and for the once-in-a-lifetime opportunities you brought into our lives. Your intelligence, intuition, and instincts kept us all relatively safe and allowed us to save countless lives. You taught us so much about animal care — from routine care to surgery and everything in between. You showed me that everyone is worth saving and that there is always more that can be done. You never gave up on an animal in need, and you taught us that love conquers all. Thank you.

I would also like to thank my talented and insightful editor, Liam, for helping me dig deeper into these stories. Thank you for turning a rough draft into a polished work for children of all ages to enjoy.

Introduction

Before I tell you about our family's pet raccoon, I guess I should tell you about my family. Having a pet raccoon doesn't make sense for most families, but it was pretty normal for us. In fact, Bandit was one of the most ordinary of our many pets.

Both Mom and Dad were school teachers, and Dad was also a pastor, so we had summer vacations together, as well as snow days and any school holidays. It made us a close family, full of laughter, love — and, of course — animals.

Everyone in our family loved animals. Mom and my older sister appreciated animals at a distance, while Dad and I loved them up close and personal. At any given time, we had two dogs and any number of more interesting animals. Life at our house was never ever boring.

I'm a third-generation animal enthusiast. Both my dad and his dad carried the gene. They both had pet alligators as young boys, both loved all kinds of animals, and both passed it on to their children.

Through the years, we had traditional pets like dogs, cats, hamsters, rabbits, fish, birds, but we also had more uncommon pets. We had wildlife, including a raccoon, deer, opossum, skunk, white squirrel, flying squirrel, snakes, silver foxes, and more. We had farm animals, including riding horses, miniature horses, milk goats, pygmy goats, cows, African pygmy pigs, and more. And we had exotic pets, including alpacas, ostriches, South American leopards, and more.

When friends hear these stories without any background on my family, they usually ask, "So, were you guys like the family in the movie *We Bought a Zoo*? How were you able to keep so many strange animals at your house?"

You might be surprised to learn that, at least at the time these stories happened, it was (usually) perfectly legal to permanently care for rescued wildlife and to raise exotic pets like ostriches and alpacas — especially in rural Virginia where we lived on almost eight acres of land. There were even exotic animal classified ads (in the *Exotic Animal Trader* magazine) and auctions, where we bought many unusual pets.

Dad was handy with tools and built some really impressive homes for the more exotic animals. My favorite was the indoor/outdoor habitat he built in our walk-out basement for three South American leopards we had at the time. To legally house them on our property, we had to have housing that conformed to some very strict guidelines for size, location, access to natural elements like trees, and so forth.

The outdoor portion of the habitat was the area outside the basement door, and we used the basement window as a bridge from the outdoor portion to the indoor portion of the habitat. The indoor habitat was a large, enclosed room, with a one-way viewing window and access door to the nesting box where the cubs were born.

What about the specialized veterinary care exotic pets require? Our local veterinarian was able and willing to help with the miniature horses, goats and pigs. For any kind of wildlife or more exotic animals, however, we were essentially on our own. We did our own vaccinations, deworming, deliveries, first aid, and even some surgeries.

Dad has always had an uncanny ability to learn new skills, almost exclusively by instinct. I always loved watching him figure out a solution and then execute it with stunning success, almost every single time. Even when it seemed nothing could be done — especially when it seemed nothing could be done — he would come up with some crazy idea, and it would work.

One quick story will help give you a window into our world. When I was about twelve years old, our cow (Bessie), fell suddenly ill and seemed by all accounts to be at death's door. In the span of a day or so, she had gone from perfectly fine to lying down in our small barn and refusing to stand or eat. Dad immediately went into veterinarian mode, checking her temperature, gum color, heartbeat, and skin for any signs of injury or illness.

When the external examination yielded no cause, we discussed every possible organ we thought could be causing her obvious discomfort and refusal to eat or stand. It was a serious situation, and she had also started refusing water. We knew without immediate relief she wouldn't make it through the night.

Dad was convinced the cause was rooted in her digestive tract somewhere, so he listened with a stethoscope we kept handy for this type of situation. He decided there was a problem with one of her stomachs. I don't know how he knew this at the time, but cows have four stomachs, or one stomach with four separate chambers (the rumen, reticulum, omasum, and abomasum). His best guess was that one of her stomachs, or stomach chambers, had herniated through the lining that held them in place. He decided that surgery was the only way to repair what he guessed was the problem.

As I recall, he called the veterinarian and asked if he would come perform the surgery, but there was talk of diagnostics to confirm Dad's diagnosis, the issue of transporting a one-and-a-half-ton cow unable to stand, and the veterinarian's rude comment about steak being the worst-case scenario. So, it was decided.

We were on our own, and we were the only chance Bessie had. Thanks to the *Davis Veterinary Supply* catalog, we had everything we needed for the surgery — anesthesia, a local anesthetic, iodine, scalpel, sterile gauze, a needle curved for sutures, sterile thread, stethoscope, surgical gloves, antibiotics, and our patient. After preparing as sterile an area as possible in the barn, we donned our surgical gloves and went to work. Some chloroform on a piece of cheesecloth was our anesthesia, and I was the anesthesiologist. Despite being only 12 years old, I was more excited than nervous. After all, this wasn't our first home surgery, and it certainly wouldn't be our last.

Despite our confidence in Dad's surgical skills, we were both worried for Bessie. She was one of the sweetest cows we'd ever had, and we couldn't bear the thought of losing her this way. She lay on a clean bed of straw topped with a clean bed sheet — sorry, Mom — with her massive head cradled in my lap.

I gently held the chloroform to her nostrils and continually listened to her heartbeat with the stethoscope. Dad had cautioned me to remove the chloroform if her heartbeat slowed too much, and we took every possible precaution.

As she drifted off to sleep, Dad applied a local anesthetic, and then quickly shaved the area for the incision. He carefully sterilized the skin with iodine, and the scalpel with heat and then iodine. With the precision of a seasoned surgeon, Dad made a quick but careful incision along Bessie's side, identifying each layer of skin, fat, muscle and membrane for my benefit as he went.

Although it was so cold we could see our breath, Dad's brow was beaded with sweat from his efforts and his intense focus on finding the hernia he believed was there. He reached through the incision into Bessie's swollen abdomen, past his gloved wrist, and blindly felt for anything out of place with Bessie's internal organs. He described every detail as he went, teaching me as he learned himself.

With one hand ready to re-apply anesthesia if Bessie's heartrate accelerated, my other hand dabbed away the blood as Dad worked. He was ecstatic when he felt a bulging area where it didn't belong. Believing the bulge to be a hernia, he carefully pushed it through the hole in the abdominal membrane and held it in place as I prepared the needle and thread.

Before the surgery began, we had sterilized the thread in alcohol, along with the needle, in preparation for this moment. I don't recall whether the thread was from Mom's stash of embroidery thread, or if it was dental floss, but it was definitely sterile. Though he wasn't particularly handy with needle and thread, Dad managed to stitch up the hernia inside simply by feeling.

The incision was barely large enough for his hands, so he couldn't see the actual hole as he stitched. Once he felt that the hernia was sufficiently closed with the errant stomach safely in place, he stitched the incision closed layer by layer. He worked backward from the internal lining that held the organs in place, to the layers of muscle, and finally, to the skin.

After he got most of the incision closed, and only lacked a dozen or so stitches on the top layer of skin, he turned the needle and thread over to me so I could finish closing the incision while he monitored the anesthesia. It wouldn't be long before Bessie started regaining consciousness, so we administered another local anesthetic to be sure she wasn't in any pain as I closed the incision.

I'm certain that when Mom taught me to cross-stitch, she never dreamed I would be using those skills to sew up the broad side of a cow, but there we were.

Though Dad's optimism was contagious, we both expected Bessie would never survive the night. Dad and I slept in the barn that night, keeping a watchful eye on our patient. Bessie had woken up from the surgery, but she was still unable to stand.

After a few hours, she was willing to drink water again, so we continued offering water and finally food until she seemed to have a bit of life about her. By daybreak, she seemed much better, eating and drinking without any apparent discomfort. By late afternoon, she stood with our help for brief periods. And by the end of the day, she was grazing in the pasture with the other cows.

Why am I telling you a cow story to introduce a book about a raccoon? I believe Bessie's story pretty much sums up what life was like with all of those animals who graced our hearts for my entire childhood. It should at least give you some idea what in the world possessed us to buy a raccoon at a gas station.

Never Buy a Raccoon at a Gas Station

Chapter 1

NEVER BUY A RACCOON AT A GAS STATION

It had been almost two weeks since my family had left for our summer vacation. After a full day of riding in the Florida and Georgia heat, our family of four, plus our two small dogs, just wanted to be home. Halfway through Georgia, it was getting dark outside, and everyone was tired, hungry, and cranky.

Dad was driving and noticed the gas tank drifting toward empty, so he pulled into the nearest gas station. Mom sat in the passenger seat and expertly performed the co-piloting duties. In addition to doling out snacks and drinks at frequent intervals, Mom was a master of precision timing with pit stops. We were well-trained to make every stop as brief as possible.

Our family's road trip rules were simple. Have your shoes on and your hand on the door handle by the time the car came to a complete stop. Go to the bathroom at every stop — whether you think you have to go or not. Throw away the car trash at every stop. The first person back to the car walks the dogs. These were the simple but effective tools that eased the strain of our frequent road trips to visit family in other states.

Within just a few minutes of the car stopping at that gas tank, Mom had gone inside with my sister, Lora, gathered all the trash from our snacks, filled the dogs' water bowl, and had taken the dogs on a quick walk. Lora wasn't far behind. She practically ran back to the car, a white 1982 Malibu Classic, still holding her nose from the filthy gas station bathroom.

I was always the slowest, so Dad had already finished pumping the gas and was headed inside to pay by the time I got my shoes on and sleepily stumbled toward the gas station bathroom, wondering what unsanitary wonders awaited me there. I was planning my strategy for scoring a Snickers and Pepsi when I noticed Dad was standing by the open window of a pickup truck talking to someone in the driver's seat.

I was around 10 years old and always curious, especially if it looked like Dad was up to something interesting. Fun fact — he usually was. He was the only person I knew who loved animals even more than I did. And this conversation had all the signs of an animal adventure.

As I got closer to where he was standing, I caught part of the conversation between my Dad and a man in the pickup truck. Dad was asking, "What would you take for it?" That's when I noticed a small moving something wrapped in a dirty blue towel on the seat beside him. I walked up to the passenger window to get a closer look.

Just as the man moved the towel to show Dad the cutest baby raccoon I'd ever seen, I heard him say, "I didn't realize I'd killed a mama coon until Old Jake found the babies in the next tree over. I got there as quickly as I could, but this little guy was the only one who survived. They couldn't be but a few weeks old."

I squealed with delight when I saw the adorable little face and tiny paws holding tightly to the man's finger. I knew what was coming even before Dad said, "We'd give him a wonderful home. Would you take twenty-five dollars for him?" I now realize the hunter probably wanted to be rid of an orphaned raccoon even more than he wanted the $25. But Dad loved to bargain, and the hunter was happy to oblige.

As I rushed over to Dad's side of the truck to meet our newest family member, Dad assured the hunter that we would take wonderful care of him and that he would live in the house with us and eat all the fresh fruits and veggies he could hold. He seemed to appreciate it and said, "I couldn't keep him anyway."

So, the deal was sealed, money was exchanged for the squirming bundle of cuteness, and we headed back to our car as the truck pulled out from the gas station.

But the real adventure had only begun. You see, when we bought that raccoon, we had no idea what a wild ride it would be. We had grossly underestimated how smoothly he would transition into our family.

For as long as I can remember, Dad always wore two shirts. He wore a white undershirt and a button-down shirt (short sleeves in summer and long sleeves in winter). His reasoning was simple. You never knew when you'd encounter an animal in need of help and there's no better way to make that initial introduction than to scoop up the animal in that top shirt, so it could feel safe, warm and protected on the way home to get it settled. I'd seen him wrap up all sorts of lost or injured animals in those shirts — snakes, squirrels, opossums, you name it.

When the hunter had handed him over, Dad had wrapped him up in his shirt like always. About 10 seconds after we got in our car and closed the doors, everyone in our car knew that we had another passenger.

The dogs noticed first, with constant sniffing getting closer and closer to Dad's shirt. Puppytee was a small, black terrier mix, and Shanda was a Pekingese.

Mom had seen the entire transaction and didn't even try to talk us out of it. Her only question was, "What kind of animal is it?" Just in case there was any doubt concerning the pet quality of a raccoon, Dad had all the bases covered.

By his logic, several facts justified this decision. First, we were already on our way home. The baby raccoon would make a wonderful pet. Raccoons are known for their cleanliness. After all, how could an animal who insists on washing every meal before eating possibly be unclean? And finally, wouldn't the baby be better off with a loving family than the hunter who had orphaned him?

Leaning over the bench seat to get a better look, my sister Lora, who was almost 14, couldn't get over how adorable he was with his bright, black button eyes and that precious little black mask around his eyes. As usual, we got a biology lesson as Dad explained that the black mask helps reduce glare and enhances raccoons' night vision, which was particularly important since they are nocturnal. "That's right," Mom said, "How are we going to get any sleep? He's going to keep us awake all night."

Dad quickly redirected the conversation to what we should name our new pet raccoon. It was a short conversation, as "Bandit" seemed the obvious choice and somehow especially fit his mischievous personality. He hadn't (yet) stolen anything or played tricks (yet), but you could see it in his eyes as plain as day.

As much as we wanted to sit there and admire how cute he was, the Georgia heat was closing in around us and we were all anxious to get back on the road so we could enjoy some much-needed air conditioning. Dad obliged and we got back on the interstate toward home.

Mom and Dad decided that Bandit should stay in the front seat away from the dogs until proper introductions could be made. Lora and I (wrongly) convinced Mom and Dad that we could handle the introductions. We were wrong.

At the exact moment that Dad handed the shirt-wrapped raccoon over the seat to Lora and me, Puppytee and Shanda identified the scent and started barking relentlessly at Bandit.

That was also the moment that all six of us learned firsthand that raccoons have a natural and incredibly effective defense mechanism when they're scared or angry. It is immediate and profound incontinence. When triggered within the confines of a small sedan with four people and two dogs on the back end of a cross-country family vacation, the result was simply overpowering. Bandit had scrambled up to the top of the back seat, seeking higher ground for his escape from the dogs. The waterfall effect was an absolute disaster.

From the floorboard of the back seat, Lora and I fought back overwhelming nausea, while Mom turned into a contortionist trying to reach the dogs to get them into the front seat so they wouldn't become part of the mess.

That was the fastest I've ever seen my dad pull over on the side of the road. Thankfully, we all still had on shoes from the recent pit stop because the moment that Malibu stopped, all of us rolled out of the car like it was full of bees. In hindsight, perhaps that's why raccoon excrement is called "scat." Trust me, if you smelled it, you'd scat too.

As we all attempted to regain our sense of smell, Dad pitched his solution, which was tying his ruined shirt (which Bandit had just turned into his own personal porta-potty) to the rear bumper of the car to "air it out." Well, that went about exactly as you might imagine, only worse, especially for the car.

Mom wisely recommended that the "solids" be removed first, and the shirt rinsed. We used the last of the water to rinse the shirt, but it was just enough to make it wetter and not enough to thoroughly clean it. Dad was confident that the rest of the mess would take care of itself on the bumper. He was wrong.

It was only at the next stop that we realized the full impact of "airing out" Dad's shirt. The drivers behind us on the interstate had undoubtedly learned the lesson before us and are probably still telling the story to this day. The next stop happened to be when we were pulled over by a state trooper.

It started with the infamous blue lights in the rearview mirror. Dad wasn't speeding, so we knew it must be about something else. As the trooper's car rolled to a stop behind our car, Mom and Dad were having a frantic discussion about the legalities of owning a raccoon in Georgia, Virginia, or anywhere else for that matter.

Holding back two barking dogs and desperately praying that Bandit didn't have an encore performance up his sleeve, Lora and I anxiously peeked through the rear window and saw the trooper approaching cautiously. Surely, we weren't going to have to give Bandit up so soon after we got him.

Very slowly, he walked from one side of the car to the other, shaking his head, before walking up to Dad's open window. I'd actually forgotten Dad's shirt was tied to the bumper until the state trooper asked Dad if he knew there was a "projectile" on the bumper.

As he leaned closer to the open car window to check the back seat, he visibly recoiled, holding a hand to his nose. Before Dad could even tell him the story, the state trooper announced with finality, "It's fine. Just go." And with that, the trooper "scatted" back to his cruiser to tell the tallest of tales, which would likely never be believed.

BANDIT'S LESSON: So, there you have it. Just like that, Bandit the raccoon joined our family. Within just a few minutes, he had made his mark with an unforgettable bathroom event that became legendary in our family. That day, my family learned the first of many lessons from Bandit — the long-term impact of an impulse decision can be life-altering.

As you'll see in the coming chapters, Bandit was not a subtle or accommodating family member. He (often literally) turned our lives upside down.

Of all the impulse decisions Dad ever made — and there were many — few had a more dramatic impact than buying a raccoon at a gas station.

Chapter 2

THE KITCHEN SINK IS NOT
FOR RACCOONS

Since he was only a few weeks old when we adopted him, Bandit quickly learned to go outside for the bathroom, following the lead of our two dogs. When he needed to go, either for the bathroom or just to play in the woods behind our house, he would scratch on the back door, and we'd let him outside. When he was ready to come home, he'd scratch on the back door to let us know he was home and inside he'd come. He slept most of the day and the back of the couch was his favorite spot.

We weren't too worried about him tracking in germs from outside, partly because it was the

1980s and people simply didn't obsess about germs like they do now. But it was mostly because Bandit was so incredibly clean. He loved to wash his hands, which was good because he was often muddy from his fishing trips in the stream behind our house. I suppose instinct took the reins when it came to his hunting trips. Like most raccoons, Bandit loved to eat fish, frogs, crawfish, and even insects.

When it was time to go fishing, Bandit would trot along beside me until we got close to the creek just beyond our backyard. Then he would run ahead so by the time I caught up, he already had his little fist deep in the mud feeling for crawfish to snack on.

After sitting by the stream watching the surface for what seemed forever, his hand would dart into the water, dive deep in the mud and come up with a crawfish or minnow in his fist. Whatever he pulled out of the stream or a hollow log, he would examine it and wash it clean in the stream before munching on it. He especially loved to bring his catch into the house with him, where he would wash it and eat it as if it were the grand prize of all time.

Bandit was our family pet for many, many years and he always kept us thoroughly entertained. We all loved him, but Mom and Bandit had a bit of a complicated relationship — kind of a love-hate situation. In Mom's defense, Bandit was an all-around scoundrel who delighted in playing pranks, especially if Mom was on the receiving end. He would hide things, play keep-away, and a host of other charades.

One of Bandit's favorite "games" to play with Mom involved him watching her for a while and then sneaking up when she wasn't looking to take whatever he had determined she most needed at the moment.

For example, if she were outside weeding a flower bed, he would watch long enough to see that she frequently reached for her gardening spade. Then, he would wait for her to step away, or even look away, long enough for him to sneak up and grab it. Then came his favorite part of the game.

He would run away with his prize and hide it somewhere for us to find later — or never. Bandit was truly a bandit in this game. He didn't even care if she caught him running away with her things. A good round of chase-the-raccoon made the game that much more fun.

His favorite thing to hide was her shoes. He had an uncanny knack for knowing exactly which shoes she most needed, and he would choose those shoes to hide. It was always a special treat when I'd find one of his hiding spots because it would always be stuffed with the most random and surprising items. One of his favorite treasure troves was a corner of my closet, where I would find small kitchen items, dog toys, Mom's shoes, Lora's cassette tapes, and whatever else caught our little Bandit's eye.

Mom loved animals and was incredibly tolerant of the endless supply of animals that invaded her home. For obvious reasons, the most resistance we ever got from Mom was whenever animals were in the kitchen. Bandit seemed to sense how protective she was of her kitchen, so he took every opportunity to exploit it.

True to a raccoon's natural instincts, Bandit was downright OCD about his food. Every day we gave him fresh fruits and vegetables in a food dish. He always washed his food before eating, and preferred a running stream of water — I guess because it was closest to the running streams he would wash food in if he'd been outside.

If he only had access to the dogs' water bowl, he would use it, but with plenty of judgmental glares in our direction to express his disapproval. His disapproval was only exceeded by the dogs' opinion on the matter.

As the only raccoon in the family, Bandit was a bit spoiled and he took full advantage of it. For a raccoon, Bandit had an incredible capacity for telling time. He never missed an opportunity to let us know it was his mealtime. Wherever we were in the house, Bandit would come to find one of us and sit up on his back legs, chattering insistently until we went to the kitchen to get his food. Perched on my shoulder and holding onto my hair for balance, he would supervise while I filled a plate with food that Mom accurately noted cost more than our own.

If Mom wasn't around, I would turn the faucet on just enough to make a steady stream. Bandit would carry one piece of food at a time to the sink to wash it under the faucet. I would put a chair in front of the sink so he could easily hop up to his wilderness stream. Cleanliness may be next to godliness, but we quickly learned that moms don't appreciate wildlife washing food in their kitchen sinks.

One day when Bandit was washing his dinner in the kitchen sink, I thought Mom was outside in the garden. I guess we lost track of time, washing and eating his carrots and blackberries and zucchini.

Bandit was perched on the edge of the sink, mostly on the countertop but close enough to the faucet that he could reach over and wash his dinner without falling into the sink. I thought we had been quite responsible, since he was sitting on a clean towel I had laid out precisely for him to sit on. I was wrong.

Mom had apparently been in the garden, picking tomatoes to go with dinner. When she walked into her clean kitchen and saw a raccoon on the countertop, she flew into action. Dropping an armful of tomatoes on the floor, Mom grabbed the broom and yelled, "Out, out, out! Get him out of here!" She marched over to the sink and turned off the water.

Bandit did not see the problem and aired his disapproval by standing up on his back feet with his two little fists in the air and chattering with all the intimidation he could muster. His plan worked and, broom or not, Mom ran into the living room.

Pleased with his performance, Bandit casually hopped to the floor, picked up a tomato to wash in the dogs' water bowl and trotted off to the living room to eat it.

That was the end of Bandit's indoor running streams, except when Mom wasn't around to see it, and he had to settle for washing his food in a bowl of water instead. He wasn't happy about losing his access to the kitchen sink, but I believe he took quite a bit of pleasure in driving the dogs crazy instead.

BANDIT'S LESSON: Bandit's devotion to hygiene, especially when it came to his food, was admirable — and even appreciated. However, there's a time and a place for everything. As we both learned that day, the time to wash his food in a running sink was not when Mom was around and the place to wash his food was *definitely* not the kitchen sink.

So, we set up a food washing station for Bandit far away from the kitchen and well-supplied with fresh water. He used it sometimes but preferred to harass the dogs by washing his food in their water bowl. What a rascal!

Chapter 3

BANDIT AND THE BOYFRIEND

If you have brothers or sisters, you know they love to annoy each other every chance they get. It was no different for my older sister and me.

During the years Bandit lived in the house with us as a pet, Lora was almost four years older than me and busy with high school, extracurricular activities and, of course, dating. She was incredibly nice to everyone, a great student, beautiful, funny, and popular. She had lots of friends who were boys and a fair number of boyfriends, so we were all accustomed to meet-and-greet protocols.

Like Bandit, I had a mischievous streak and loved to play a good prank any chance I got. Lora's steady stream of boyfriends made easy targets. They always entered our home on their best behavior, well aware that Dad was a local pastor, teacher and protective father. Their good natures extended to me, as they would pretend not to be annoyed by my juvenile antics, but we all knew it was mostly part of the show.

With a partner in crime like Bandit, the sky was the limit. Normally, my harassment consisted of assigning the boyfriend a clever nickname and then making sure I was in the way as much as possible. But on special occasions, Bandit and I would go all out.

The typical boyfriend smell could be overwhelming at times, as they were practically dripping with 80's colognes like Polo, Obsession, and Drakkar. Some wore boat shoes and khakis with turned-up shirt collars, while others wore football jerseys with jeans and tennis shoes. Others wore cowboy boots and jeans, or camouflage jackets and hiking boots.

Whatever they wore, it was always the same routine.

One night we had just finished eating and cleaning the kitchen when Lora excused herself to go get ready for her date, who was to arrive in an hour. That didn't give us much time, but we'd done more with less. The plan was to lure the date into a false sense of security while he waited for Lora to come downstairs — and then — *bam!* A Bandit-themed surprise!

Lora was upstairs finishing her hair and makeup, blasting "Flashdance" and Michael Jackson's "Billie Jean." I knew within minutes her date (we'll call him Nate) would arrive in a cloud of Polo cologne, and a few minutes after that she would descend the stairs in a cloud of White Rain hairspray. What can I say? It was the 80s.

Bandit and I were ready to make an unforgettable entrance. He loved meeting new people and usually approved of everyone he met. That's one of many reasons the next several minutes took us all by surprise. Bandit and I were sitting at the bottom of the stairs, and the front door was behind us on the other side of the house.

We were right where we needed to be — between Lora and her date. Between us and the front door was Dad, who was watching even more eagerly for Nate's arrival. We were all ready. Without realizing it, Dad was our accomplice as he always talked to the boyfriends before they left the house.

There it was — the crunch of gravel in the driveway, a car door closing, the knock on the door, the nervous clearing of the throat, the open door and then — yep — the cloud of Polo cologne. We could smell it all the way on the other side of the house within seconds of Nate's walking into the living room.

Dad invited him to have a seat, assuring him Lora would be down any minute. They chatted about the usual dad-and-date stuff like curfew and guns while Lora worked double-time to get downstairs as quickly as possible, ideally before Dad could scare her date away.

Upstairs her bedroom door opened, and we could smell the hairspray headed our way. This was it. It was time! I motioned for Bandit to stay at the edge of the living room while I went in to say hi. You should have seen his face when I asked him if Lora had told him about our pet raccoon. Pet raccoon?! She had not.

As if on cue, Bandit bounded into the room and sat on the floor right in front of Nate, as if sizing him up. Bandit's intelligent little face swept up and down and then again. With one quick glance my way, Bandit leaped right into Nate's lap. The only reaction Nate had time for was a quick, "What in the world?!" Dad and I both knew what was coming next, and so did Lora, who was just then rounding the corner to see the scene.

At that moment, several things happened at exactly the same time. Nate acted first, jumping up from his seat almost immediately after Bandit landed in his lap full of disapproval, mischief and his fully-armed defense mechanism. As Nate jumped up, Dad lunged toward Bandit, landing on the floor just short of the couch. Sitting on the other end of the couch with an empty seat between Nate and me, I lunged for Bandit to keep him from falling on the floor.

I caught him just in time to pull him onto the couch between my seat and Nate's. That's when Lora screamed, "Get him out of here!" That's also the exact moment that Bandit triggered his favorite defense mechanism — immediate and extreme diarrhea.

Though he had jumped up in time to clear the blast zone, Nate was sufficiently traumatized by the scene on the couch. His first reflex was to check his hair, a neatly feathered blonde mullet. Needless to say, the couch was ruined, along with their date.

Judging by his response to being run over by Bandit's welcome wagon, Nate was not a good candidate for our family anyway. If a raccoon spooked him, he would never have survived the rest of our animals.

That single, defining moment triggered an immediate and permanent departure of the boyfriend. With one final flick of his turned-up pink polo shirt collar, Nate turned on his heel, spun out of the driveway in his silver Mustang and never ever came back.

Lora ran after him, but it was no use. She came back in, took one look at the scene in the living room, and ran upstairs sobbing. She was furious. Dad was stunned for just a second, and then we both fell over laughing at what had just happened. Sure, there was one whopper of a mess to clean up, but Bandit had single-handedly done what Dad wished he could have done. A boyfriend had never ever been so efficiently removed from our home. I believe he may even have said, "Good boy, Bandit!"

Bandit showed absolutely no remorse for what he'd done, but boy, was he ever proud. He was grinning ear to ear as he jumped into Dad's arms. Somehow, I think Dad didn't mind cleaning up that awful mess. Some things are worth the mess.

I'd like to tell you that Bandit was reformed and improved his manners, but he did not. Though that reaction was the most extreme, he continued to delight in harassing Lora's friends and boyfriends every chance he got.

BANDIT'S LESSON: Though I never knew of any specific reason that Nate was unqualified to be Lora's boyfriend, I've always wondered if he sensed something we missed. Perhaps he was just having some good, not-so-clean fun. Or perhaps he was saving her from heartbreak down the road.

The moral of the story? Everyone should have a friend who is a great judge of character and who is not afraid to express their opinions.

Chapter 4

OPEN CAR DOOR, INSERT RACCOON

During the years that we had Bandit, we lived in Virginia near my mom's side of the family, and most school holidays were spent in Florida with my dad's side of the family. It was a long drive, but it kept us close to both sides of the family. And who doesn't love a good 12-hour road trip in a 4-door sedan with 4 people and 2 dogs? Do the math. It's not pretty.

Since the disaster of his first road trip with us, Bandit had never been invited on a second. He ran quick errands in the car with us, but none of us wanted the drama of his company in the car for another full-on road trip.

Instead, Bandit had stayed at home with free access to his treetop wooden house Dad had built for him, enjoying the comfort of the small barn where the goats stayed, along with wherever else he wanted to roam. We always left him a supply of food and treats in the goat barn, along with fresh water, though I suspect he preferred the stream behind the house.

One hot summer night, our family had just pulled into our driveway from a long summer vacation in Florida. We were all exhausted, cranky and desperate to get inside and sleep in our own beds. So, as soon as the car stopped in the driveway, Dad practically leaped out of the passenger seat to unload the trunk while Lora and I gathered our assortment of trip supplies into what would hopefully be one trip from the car to the house.

Dad had the same rules for unloading that he had for loading. It was pretty simple. If you wanted your stuff to go on the trip with you, it was your responsibility to bring your suitcase (one per person) out to the car. Each suitcase was placed by the trunk but not in it. Packing the trunk was an intricate game of Tetris that Dad had mastered years before someone translated trunk-packing into a video game. The same was true of the unpacking. Dad unloaded it all from the trunk and put it on the ground by the car for us to take our own things inside. If you didn't bring it inside, it stayed outside.

Lora and I were arguing over who should have to take the blankets inside since I had used them last. We were trying to find the Simon game whose beeping was coming from somewhere under the seat.

Simon was an awesome handheld game — a pioneer in the electronic games industry — that had four colored sections (red, blue, green and yellow) that would light up in a particular pattern. The goal of the game was to repeat the pattern by pushing the colored buttons in the right order. Looking back, it was a simple game, but without more interesting electronics to compete for our attention, it was entertaining enough to keep us mostly agreeable for hours at a time. It likely had an entirely different effect on our parents.

Between the noise of Simon's persistent beeping, our arguing, Dad's unloading instructions, and Mom's peacemaking it was a real scene.

Dad had taken a load inside the house already and had, on the same trip inside, moved the dogs in from the car to the house. Lora was headed inside with a load of her stuff. We were each allowed one suitcase and one car bag, though Dad had made an exception for Lora's Caboodle.

In the 80s, every girl had a Caboodle to organize the myriad hair scrunchies, makeup and big, brightly-colored, acrylic jewelry. As Lora headed upstairs to her room with her suitcase, Caboodle and purse, the dogs headed back outside and immediately started barking as if their lives depended on it.

Mom had driven the last part of the trip and, I'm sure, couldn't wait to get inside and go to bed. About the time the barking dogs charged toward the car, she opened her car door for some fresh air (you know that familiar road trip smell) and leaned across the front seat to the passenger floorboard to retrieve her purse and the family snack bag.

A moment later, Mom threw both hands up in the air and let loose a bloodcurdling scream. Snacks flew in all directions as the rest of the family ran to see what had caused the scream, which was still going strong. I'm not sure how she managed a breath between the screams.

Since the dome light in the car was turned off for the trip, Dad had to grab a flashlight from the trunk to see what in the world was happening. As our eyes adjusted to the dark and to the flashlight's beam, there sat Mom with her hands up in the air, screaming. She was face-to-face with Bandit, who was sitting in her lap with his hands up in the air just like her.

One of Bandit's favorite greetings was to stand up on his back feet with his two little front feet in the air. He'd make a happy little squealy, chirpy sound as if he were trying to say, "Hi there. I really missed you!" I guess he had really, really missed us because that was one doozy of a greeting. When Bandit saw us and the barking dogs, he hopped out of the car and up into my arms. It's a miracle he didn't trigger his defense mechanism all over me as the dogs barked, Mom screamed, and Dad doubled over, laughing.

I don't remember how long it took for Mom to regain her composure enough to climb out of the car. I'm sure she was instantly wide awake, though. And from that day on, she always, always looked to see what was on the other side of her open car door.

BANDIT'S LESSON: After such a long and crowded road trip, I'm quite sure Mom never expected the greeting she got in the driveway that night. In your wildest imagination, would you expect a raccoon to jump into your car and onto your lap?

Bandit taught us all never to underestimate what might be hiding just out of sight. It might be something amazing that you never saw coming — a long-lost friend or unexpected job opportunity.

Or it might be a raccoon in your lap.

Chapter 5

BANDIT GOES TO SCHOOL

Not many things strike fear in a middle schooler's heart like being called to the principal's office — especially if you brought your pet raccoon to school with you that day. But there I was, standing in the principal's office with Bandit perched on my shoulder, holding my braid for balance. Thankfully, this wasn't a traditional "trip to the principal's office" but more of a friendly visit since it wasn't a school day and I was there helping my dad, who was a teacher there.

The day had started with an early morning knock on my bedroom door. Early mornings were tough for me even when it's expected, like on a school day. But this was three whole days before school started. This was what all kids lived for — the last precious days of summer break. Dad knocked and popped his head in to announce that I was going to school with him to help get his classroom ready.

If your parents are teachers, you know that just because school is out for students doesn't necessarily mean that you get a day off. It was a dreaded "teacher workday" and our parents, both teachers, usually "invited" Lora and me to help them. Mom taught sixth grade at one school and Dad taught first grade at another school. Lora had already left with Mom to help get her class ready, so I was supposed to go with Dad to help him get his room ready.

Although it was far too early for my liking, it was usually pretty fun helping Dad do anything. He turned everything into an adventure. I knew from last night's dinner conversation that he was planning to build a reading loft in his classroom, and that sounded fun. But it wasn't fun enough to get me out of bed this early.

That all changed when Dad announced, "Why don't we bring Bandit with us?" Bandit was curled up under the covers, resting from another busy night of raiding my closet. He ran to the door when he heard his name. "Really? Can we really take him to school?" I said, bounding out of bed like it was noon. Dad reminded me that since it was summer, only teachers and the principal would be there. So, we all got ready for school — Bandit's first ever day of school.

As soon as we were dressed and ready, we got Bandit ready with a quick bath in the sink (good thing Mom wasn't home to see it), a good brushing, and a bag of fresh fruits and veggies to keep him occupied while we worked. It was a little insulting that he washed his hands after we finished giving him a bath. As he washed his hands, he looked at us in disapproval, as if to say, *"You missed a spot."*

In those days Bandit was almost always in the house with us since he was as close to domesticated as a raccoon can expect to be. He even wore a small dog collar and a flea collar.

We had recently started training him to walk on a leash, but he was not a fan. He was plenty smart enough to know what we wanted him to do, but also smart enough to avoid doing anything that he didn't want to do. Still, it was fun to try.

So, all three of us headed to the car just like it was any normal school day. This, however, would not be normal at all. Bandit would see to that.

When we got to school, Bandit must have sensed adventure ahead. He was ready for his first day of school! He hopped out of the car and bounded along beside me, wearing his leash with all the composure of a show dog. When we stepped inside, Bandit climbed up to my shoulder and stayed there until we got to Dad's classroom.

Once inside the classroom, we closed the door so Bandit could freely explore. Boy, did he ever. He must have picked up and examined every pencil, crayon and glue bottle in the place. He sat in the chairs, climbed the curtains, and had a wonderful time. After a while, he took a break to snack on some carrots we had brought. Dad put a bowl of water on the table for him and he carefully washed each carrot before eating it.

When it was time for us to start building the reading loft, Bandit was ready to help. Mostly, he hid tools and nails from Dad, but at least he wasn't making a mess. Yet. Since he was nocturnal, he quickly tired of "helping" and curled up on a blanket for a nap.

The reading loft was made of wooden boards that created a raised platform about four feet off the ground, with a short set of stairs leading to the top. The platform was tucked securely into a corner of the room and secured to both walls for safety. We hung curtains from the base of the platform to create a reading nook underneath with bookshelves, beanbags, and lamps.

It took most of the day to build, and when we were done, Bandit was happy to inspect our work. He climbed the bottom curtains, up to the top rails, where he walked every inch of the top level. On top of the rails, he looked out over the whole classroom. Satisfied, he curled up on a beanbag down below for another nap.

While Bandit napped, Dad and I hung posters, organized classroom supplies, cleaned and did all the workday things that teachers do. We had packed ourselves a lunch to avoid taking Bandit around too many people. As soon as we unwrapped the first sandwich, there was Bandit, awake and ready to beg for more food.

After our late lunch, Dad decided we had done enough for one day. He needed to get home to clean the pool and mow the lawn. And we knew Bandit would be ready for a bathroom break outside. So, we headed to the office to let the principal know that we were heading home for the day.

You may wonder what in the world we were thinking when we walked a raccoon into an office full of people. I think we weren't thinking at all. Dad and I both had seen how Bandit reacted when he was scared or just didn't like someone. We should have known better, but we didn't.

The reactions in the office were kind of like an ocean wave that starts far away as a tiny ripple and swells to a huge wave crashing on the shore. The first to notice Bandit, who was by now back on my shoulder, was the school secretary, Ms. Horner. She was the furthest from us but was, by far, the most terrified. She jumped up onto her chair and screamed, looking for all the world like my Mom does every time Bandit surprises her in the house. She was the ripple that started the wave crashing toward us.

Two other teachers and the principal stood nearby. When Ms. Horner screamed, they immediately looked where she was pointing and saw Bandit. By this time, Bandit was as scared of Ms. Horner as she was of him. He was clutching a fistful of my braid and hanging on for dear life.

Just as I turned to get Bandit out of there, the principal, Mr. Martin, said, "Hold on. Let's see this little guy." I looked at Dad, who nodded his approval. So, Mr. Martin came over and for a moment it seemed like the introduction would be uneventful after all.

Just then, Mr. Martin reached his hand toward Bandit. The very next moment ended the introduction in a way only Bandit could manage. In that split second, my pet raccoon had ruined my clothes, the office floor, and any chance he'd ever had of attending school.

We made a hasty exit, promising to clean up the mess just as soon as we got Bandit outside. That was Bandit's first and last day of school.

Thankfully, that trip to the principal's office was more of a friendly visit, with no disciplinary agenda. I was a pretty good kid, who mostly followed the rules except for being too chatty in the classroom. A trip to the principal's office for a legitimate rule violation was rare indeed.

Long before that day, an animal had sent me to the office for the hysteria I had caused my third-grade teacher, Miss Marble. At that time, the guidelines for show-and-tell were far less restrictive than they are today. It was kind of an anything-goes, hope-for-the-best approach.

Miss Marble was a kind but rather high-strung woman. She was tall and thin with short, red hair and bright blue eyes. She had spent most of the school year trying to teach me to pay attention in class, which was hard to do when I had so much to talk about with my classmates.

She even had me skip PE for a whole month to stay in the classroom and read the story titled "Lucy Didn't Listen" in my reading book. It was the best month of the year. I hated PE and I loved to read.

Show & Tell Day was the highlight of the week for most of us, and it afforded Miss Marble a few precious minutes of vaguely paying attention while we presented our most prized artifacts. Mostly, she graded papers during this time and looked up often enough to announce the next presenter. Perhaps that's why she didn't notice what I'd brought until it was too late.

A few of my friends had already presented their treasures by the time Dad knocked on the classroom door, holding a small brown paper bag. He told Miss Marble he had brought my

Show & Tell items, and she casually waved him over to where I was seated.

Dad helped me with the showing and telling. He told my class the story of Medusa from Greek and Roman mythology. Still, Miss Marble didn't look up from grading papers.

When the story advanced to the point where Medusa's hair — a headful of snakes — was described, Miss Marble seemed to sense that something of interest was happening. She looked up just as Dad was reaching into the bag. As he pulled something from the bag, he got Miss Marble's full attention.

From her desk, she only saw a fellow teacher with a brown paper bag, so she wasn't at all suspicious as she started walking toward us to get a closer look. What Dad now held in his hands was a writhing bundle of tightly-coiled, bright green garden snakes. The baby snakes were tiny — about the size of a large earthworm, and I thought they were adorable.

By this time, Dad was describing how Medusa's snake hair would have looked. He said, "Snakes are cold-blooded reptiles, so they love to get warm anywhere they can find a heat source. One of their favorite places to snuggle up is in long hair." At that point, he placed the bundle of baby snakes on top of my head and they did indeed wind their way into and under my long, straight hair, peeking out just like Medusa's snakes might have.

That was the exact moment that Miss Marble got close enough to clearly see that her classroom was being visited by not one, but *dozens* of live snakes. In the very next moment, she screamed the loudest, longest, most terrifying scream I've ever heard.

She ran to her desk, jumped on top of it and continued to scream while Dad and I did our best to round up all the snakes that had fallen to the floor. As soon as they touched the cold floor, they scattered in all directions. Some were still in my hair, so I put them back in the bag while come classmates helped Dad pick up snakes from under furniture, behind bookcases and everywhere else they had run for cover.

At last, we had collected most, if not all, of the snakes, and Dad had taken them to safety.

Miss Marble was still on her desk screaming, as were several of my classmates. Everyone else had had a grand time on the snake round-up. It had taken us forever to (hopefully) find all the snakes and collect them, and it took even longer for my poor teacher to recover her senses enough to send me to the office.

After that day, strict rules were imposed for what could and could not be brought into school for show-and-tell. I guess Mr. Martin didn't realize how fortunate he was with Bandit's memorable visit. At least he was just one animal.

BANDIT'S LESSON: As we learned that day in the principal's office, what may seem like the best possible idea can end in disaster if you don't think it through. That morning when Dad suggested that we bring Bandit, neither of us imagined that his visit would end in such a mess — although we shouldn't have been too surprised, considering that was Bandit's default defense mechanism.

We also failed to see beyond our own limited reality of what it's like having a raccoon for company. The things to which we grow accustomed fail to get our attention at all, but they can be so apparent to others less familiar with our perceived reality. Bandit taught us to think before we acted and to see a situation from others' perspectives before deciding on a course of action. Perhaps that's why he never visited school again.

Chapter 6

BANDIT THE SURPRISE TEDDY BEAR

While Bandit lived in the house with us, he was free to come and go as he pleased, but he usually chose to be in the house with us. He learned by watching our two dogs and scratched on the door to go outside for bathroom breaks. He (sort of) walked on a leash when necessary. And he napped on the couch or in the bed, snuggled under blankets like a real, live teddy bear.

Bandit wore a collar, got regular baths (mostly initiated by him — he loved playing in the water), and developed relatively good manners. Most days, he and I would walk down to the creek behind our house for him to hunt frogs, crawfish, fish and anything else that looked appetizing to him. Like all raccoons, he washed everything he ate and took a great deal of pride in his appearance. He would sit for ages in the creek, washing his adorable little face and hands.

When it was bedtime, he went outside with the dogs for one last bathroom trip before trotting upstairs to my room. By the time I'd brushed my teeth and gotten ready for bed each night, Bandit would be all curled up in my bed, sound asleep.

Raccoons are soft and snuggly bed buddies, but there's one big problem. They're nocturnal. So, every night Bandit would catch a quick power nap with me and then he was ready to explore. We quickly learned how important it was for me to keep my bedroom door closed. At least that way Bandit's adventures were confined to one room. I was a sound sleeper, so I didn't mind. In the morning, I got to pick up all the stuff he'd pulled out to play with. By then, Bandit would be back in bed, sound asleep.

One night when I got into bed, I noticed Bandit wasn't there. Figuring he must still be outside with the dogs, I lay down with a book and waited for him to come to bed. I must have dozed off because the next thing I remember was Mom's scream — what became known as her "Bandit scream" — coming from her bedroom.

I jumped out of bed and raced in that direction, meeting Dad and Lora on the way. We arrived at the master bedroom just in time to see Mom crouched in the corner screaming and Bandit standing up on the foot of the bed, chattering furiously at her. He looked like a tiny, furry preacher in the pulpit, as he furiously bobbed up and down, waving his tiny fists in the air.

To fully appreciate the scene we walked into that night, you should know a bit more about Mom's relationship with Bandit. First of all, my mom is the kindest, gentlest soul who has ever breathed. She loves all people and all animals, but she also has enough common sense to recognize that some animals do not belong in the house — or the car, for that matter.

Ever since their road trip introduction, Bandit seemed to sense her reservations about having a raccoon for a pet. Instead of trying to win her over, however, he seized every opportunity to torment her with his pranks. I'm not sure if he thought it was a game that he won every time he was able to produce Mom's hallmark "Bandit scream," or if he just delighted in making her jump and run. Whatever his motivation was, Mom was most definitely his favorite target.

So, there we all were in Mom and Dad's bedroom, with Mom crouched in the corner of her bedroom, yelling, "Get that creature out of here!" Both dogs were hiding under the bed, while Dad, Lora, and I stood in the doorway laughing at the scene but also coaxing Bandit away from his fiery sermon, which he had directed at Mom. He still stood at the foot of the bed and was quite agitated. When we caught our breath from laughing so hard, Dad and I called to Bandit with a firm, "Bandit, come!"

He looked once in our direction and once in Mom's before he bounded off the bed to the floor. That, of course, elicited another scream from Mom as he faked one step in her direction, as if to say, "I could sleep here if I really wanted to." And then, as quickly as the dramatic scene had started, it ended.

Without another word from anyone, Bandit raced out of the room and headed toward my room. He was, after all, a very smart raccoon. By the time Mom had regained her senses enough to find Bandit and put him outside, he was already sound asleep under my covers. If it's possible for a raccoon to play opossum, he definitely was, probably quite pleased with another successful prank on Mom.

BANDIT'S LESSON: I suppose Bandit's big lesson that particular night was to always check under the covers. At least, that's what Mom took from it, as she always checked under the covers after that night. Perhaps the larger lesson was thinking a few steps ahead wherever you are. See the situation you're in, but also see what could be just ahead. Is it an exciting opportunity you might otherwise miss? Or is it a random surprise — like a raccoon under the covers?

Chapter 7

THAT'S NOT A MONKEY ON YOUR BACK

Some of our family's funniest and most unforgettable memories are thanks to Bandit and his hilarious personality. There's a saying that goes something like, "You can take the girl out of the country, but you can't take the country out of the girl." I believe the same is true of domesticated wildlife. In Bandit's case, at least, we took the raccoon out of the wild, but we never took the wild out of the raccoon.

Deep down we all had a feeling that Bandit's time with us might be limited. The years that he lived inside with us weren't nearly long enough for Dad and me, but for Mom and Lora, it was just fine. As much as we loved his company, and he loved ours, domesticating wildlife is not always the best idea.

Sure, he was housetrained and kept himself quite clean. He drank out of the dogs' water bowls, ate when they ate, played in the yard with the other animals, and even slept in my bed. In so many ways, it was like having a very playful cat or exceptionally agile dog. But he reminded us in so many ways that he was still a wild animal with different drives and ideas about house life.

The traces of wild instinct that lingered in Bandit broke through at the most random times. The effect was surprising, and usually quite comical. The first time we caught him washing his food in the dogs' water bowl was one of those moments. It wasn't expected at first, but then it made perfect sense. Of course, raccoons wash their food in the wild. We just didn't expect to see it happen in our house.

I've often wondered if his pranks were the result of instinct more than mischief. But then

I remember the twinkle in his eye — and what looked for all the world like a smile every time he played a prank — and I think otherwise.

The other indicator of intentional mischief was the way Bandit singled out my mom as his favorite target. He had to know that she cared about him. After all, Mom was about the nicest, most generous person I've ever known, even to animals who probably belonged outdoors. I think he picked up on the fact that she wasn't on board with a raccoon living under her roof and either wanted to win her over or wanted to make her regret it. Or maybe he was just a scamp.

One of the funniest examples of Bandit's wild instincts breaking through is the day he welcomed my mom home from the grocery store by leaping from the curtain rod onto her back. The next few minutes are a bit of blur because everything happened so fast, but to the best of our recollection, it went like this.

Bandit loved to be up high — at the top of a tree, riding on our shoulders, lying on the back of the couch, or on this fateful day, perched on a curtain rod right beside the front door. Mom was well aware Bandit would likely be in the house when she got home, but I doubt she expected what happened next.

Bandit was indeed in the house. In fact, he had heard Mom's car pull in the driveway and had quickly scaled the curtains to sit in wait at the end of the curtain rod, as close as possible to the door she was about to open.

After a long day of teaching middle school, Mom had stopped by the store for groceries so she could rush home to make dinner for the family. Dad was outside feeding the horses and goats. Lora and I were (supposed to be) upstairs in our rooms, doing our homework. Instead, Lora was in her room and I was in the living room half-heartedly practicing for my weekly piano lesson, when the front door opened.

What immediately followed was a bloodcurdling scream the likes of which none of us had ever heard. Lora and I dropped everything and ran toward the commotion, not sure what to expect.

When we rounded the corner, the first thing we saw was a heap of groceries on the floor, bursting from the broken seams of brown paper grocery bags. As apples and grapes — Bandit's favorite — rolled to a stop at our feet, Mom screamed, "Aaahhhhh!!!! Get this creature off of me!!!" but Mom was long gone. As we ran into the kitchen, we saw two things.

First, we saw Mom running faster than we knew she could, circling the kitchen table over and over as her arms flailed to shake the delighted prankster off of her back. Then we saw the look on Bandit's face as he hung onto her jacket for dear life, looking for all the world like a rodeo rider. He grinned from ear to ear as he finally jumped off her back, to the kitchen table and then to the floor.

That's when the real chase began. Bandit noted the direction in which Mom was running and headed her off, so she had to change course with him in hot pursuit, practically on her heels. He obviously meant no harm beyond a fun game of chase, but Mom was not convinced.

They must have run around that table a dozen times before Mom gained enough of a lead to break off in the direction of the stairs. Lora and I followed close behind, uselessly calling Bandit to come. He was having far too much fun to stop now.

Mom climbed the stairs two at a time, and Bandit took three. By the time she reached the top of the stairs, he was just a step or two behind. Mom had a decision to make. Turn right at the top of the stairs and take refuge in the master bedroom — or turn left and risk making it all the way down the hallway to the bathroom.

She opted for the bedroom since it was closest and slammed the door in Bandit's face just as he leaped after her. Not to be deterred, Bandit frantically scratched at the bedroom door while Mom continued screaming for help.

By the time Lora and I got upstairs, Bandit was sitting on the floor outside the door, scratching and smiling for all he was worth. I scooped him up into my arms and scolded him for what he'd done, but I'm sure he didn't regret it for one second.

If it's possible for a raccoon to laugh, I am 100% certain that Bandit laughed all the way to the back door. That was the day we built Bandit a treehouse and he became an indoor/outdoor raccoon.

Yes, when Mom walked in the door that day, she probably expected lots of things, but a raccoon pouncing onto her back from the curtain rod was almost certainly not among them. I believe after that day, she always made it a habit to look both ways and, perhaps most importantly, to look up.

BANDIT'S LESSON: It wasn't news to us that Bandit was a wild animal no matter how long he had lived in the house. But that day, Bandit taught us an important lesson on awareness.

When Mom walked through that front door, I'm sure she had no idea at all that Bandit was sitting above her, ready to pounce. We all learned how important it is to always be aware of your surroundings. Living at our house was a constant exercise in expecting the unexpected and rolling with whatever came our way.

Chapter 8

BANDIT'S NEW HOUSE

Immediately after he treed Mom in her bedroom, Bandit had become an indoor/outdoor raccoon, complete with a luxury penthouse Dad had built for him and mounted in a tall tree overlooking Bandit's favorite part of the creek.

While other raccoons had to settle for ground-level dens harassed by coyotes, bobcats and other predators, Bandit had the advantage of height with his treetop condo. His only real predator up there would be large owls or hawks, but Dad made Bandit's house plenty deep enough and with a small enough hole that he could enter without fear of a predator.

The decision to begin Bandit's transition back to the wild was a hard-fought battle that I lost in the end. He was my best buddy, my sidekick, my partner in crime. After even the toughest school days, I knew I'd find him asleep on my bed or the couch, waiting for us to get home to play.

Growing up in the country, we had lost animals to illness or injury — or most often, old age — but this was something else entirely. After all, it's not every day your house pet moves out into his own home to start a family of his own.

Knowing it wasn't "goodbye" but "see you around" made it easier. His outdoor home was within sight of our back door, and it was nice knowing that he was so close. Mom and Lora appreciated that there was a closed door between them and Bandit since they were frequent targets of his pranks.

We all agreed that he was welcome to come inside and visit whenever he wanted to, for as long as he wanted to. It was easy since he already knew to scratch on the door when he wanted to go out or come in.

On the day his outdoor home was ready, Dad climbed the tree that held his house and called Bandit up beside him to show him his new front door. After a little sniffing of the fresh-cut wood and the pine needle bedding inside, Bandit scooted through the small, round opening and peeked out at us happily. He was home!

Dad climbed down the tree, and we headed back inside, sad but also excited for Bandit's new opportunities to start a family. As I followed Dad inside the house, something darted past us. Bandit had followed us inside, not quite ready for his newfound independence. In the coming days, he spent more time each day in his new home, even taking household items to make it a bit more comfortable.

I don't remember how many years we had Bandit, after that first year in the house, but it was quite a few, and he always came back to visit. He scratched on the door when he needed to go in or out, reserving his "accidents" for guests he disliked.

After growing up indoors, he had long since made his peace with our dogs, so his visits consisted of a scratching on the back door, and a quick exploration of the house before returning to our laps for some snuggles. We could always count on a scratch on the door when it stormed or got too cold, even if it was only for the briefest of visits. He seemed content to check in once in a while to let us know he was okay.

When he first moved out, he would stay in his outdoor house for a few days at a time, and then he'd be back inside with us for a few days. The days became weeks and then months; soon he was outside more than he was inside. Just when Mom and Lora thought he was gone for good, there would be a little scratch on the back door and in he'd trot.

One spring day when he'd been gone for several months, Bandit scratched on the back door but refused to come in the house. I stepped outside to greet him, but he didn't seem as silly as usual. He would run a few steps toward the edge of the woods behind our house and then run back to me. I decided to follow him each time he'd run ahead, and soon we were at the edge of the creek. I saw his footprints by the creek, but I also saw smaller footprints. Bandit was a dad! I ran to get Dad so he could help me find Bandit's family (baby raccoons!!!!).

Dad was feeding the horses, and by the time he was able to follow me to the edge of the woods, Bandit was standing there waiting for us. We called him, and he wouldn't come over like he used to. He also didn't try to run away. We walked all the way to where he was standing, and he let us talk to him and pet him just like always.

Then he turned toward the tree where we'd built his home a few years earlier. As he approached the tree, there was a rustling in the leaves that could only have been his family. We never got to meet his family, but I'll always believe that was his goodbye to us. I think he wanted us to know that he was happy and well with a family of his own.

Dad looked at me and said, "Well, I believe that's the last we'll see of Bandit for a good long while." He was right. Other than a few random visits, Bandit had moved on to the next and final chapters of his life. He may have moved out and then moved on, but he left an indelible mark on our hearts and in our family's memories.

As much as I loved our dogs and other pets, there was a special bond with Bandit. Maybe it was because he was only a few weeks old when he joined our family. Maybe it was because I gave him all the fresh fruits and veggies he wanted. Whatever the reason, he was special.

BANDIT'S LESSON: This was perhaps the biggest lesson we learned from Bandit — if you love someone, you put their needs before your own. As much as we wanted to keep him inside as a fully domesticated pet, it wasn't necessarily the best place for him. It wouldn't have been fair to keep him from starting his own life with a family of his own. He might not have known what he was missing, but we would have known.

In the end, I'm glad we gave him the outdoor option and gave him such a smooth transition. The joy we got from watching him raise his sweet little family in the wild far outweighed the sadness. We loved him enough to let him go.

Epilogue

If you were even remotely entertained by these Bandit stories, I believe you'll really enjoy my next book. It tells the stories of several other unusual pets we had growing up, including leopards, alpacas, an opossum, a skunk, miniature pigs, miniature horses, silver foxes, a deer and more.

In the next book, you'll meet our pet opossum, Harriet. From Harriet, we learned that when things aren't found where you expect them to be, the results can be surprising and can have dramatically negative consequences. Everyone within hearing distance of my mom's scream learned this lesson the afternoon she opened a kitchen drawer for a dish towel and found a shocking surprise instead.

You'll also meet our pet margay, Baque, who taught me an important lesson when I walked into his indoor/outdoor habitat to feed him his evening meal (an entire raw chicken). The first lesson is probably not to enter the habitat of a leopard. In this case, I was counting on the fact that we had hand-raised Baque since he was a tiny cub and he was normally very affectionate. I was wrong.

If you prefer even more danger, you'll love the 5-foot-long alligator who taught my dad an important lesson the day he lifted the alligator into the rear window of the family sedan. On a family drive, he, my mom and my sister had seen the alligator on the side of the road completely still and apparently hit by a car.

Having had a pet alligator as a young boy, Dad had a soft spot for alligators and decided its death should at least serve a purpose. When he put it in the back seat of the car with my sister, who was about 3 years old, his plans included an alligator belt, boots, maybe an amateur venture into taxidermy, who really knows? His plans most certainly did not include what happened several minutes later.

Or perhaps you prefer sweeter, more inspirational stories? You'll love our silver foxes, George and Emily, who taught me infinite patience. I bought them for $35 from someone who had trapped them in the wild. They were rightfully scared of humans and in hindsight I should have released them as soon as I bought their freedom.

Instead, Dad helped me build them a big, beautiful habitat complete with tree branches and all sorts of cool nature stuff. It was plenty big enough for us to walk around inside and I decided that my mission that summer would be to tame my foxes so they could live inside with us like our dogs. It was a mission (sort of) accomplished.

From the time I was born until I left home for college, animals were such an important part of our family. We learned so much from each and every one, and the lessons were so random and surprising. The overwhelming theme of our animal adventures was a deep love and respect for what made each animal so special.

We learned responsibility as we fed and cared for them in all seasons, at the most inconvenient times, and putting their needs ahead of our own. We learned the value of collaboration and teamwork as we worked together, as a family and with other friends in the exotic animal community, to solve the inevitable problems that come with so many animals.

And we learned perseverance. Often the fun turned to fear, as we struggled to save an ill or injured pet. Sometimes, even the veterinarian would give up on the animal (try convincing a veterinarian to perform a C-section on a miniature pig on Christmas Eve), but we never did. Dad always persisted until we either solved the problem or knew that we had done everything that could possibly be done. That's how I learned to perform CPR on a horse.

I'm excited to share the next round of stories with you, as we live and learn together.

To get the latest updates, join my mailing list at:

https://bit.ly/2QSv4VK

Until then...

Never buy a raccoon at a gas station.

About the Author

Beth Detjens enjoyed an extraordinary childhood in rural Virginia, where her family hosted an endless menagerie of domestic pets, exotic pets, and local wildlife. In addition to domestic pets like horses, dogs, and goats, Beth's family raised exotic pets like leopards, alpacas, ostriches, and miniature horses/pigs/goats — and wildlife including a raccoon, opossum, skunks, squirrels, snakes, a deer, and foxes.

Beth has earned two Bachelor's Degrees — first in Secondary English Education and later in Exceptional Student Education. Her two Master's Degrees are in business — a Master of Arts in Business Administration (MBA) and a Master of Science in Management and Leadership (MSML). Today, Beth enjoys a corporate career in marketing, along with freelance writing, graphic design, and business consulting.

She appreciates the simple joys of family life with her husband, two amazing kids, and two Goldendoodles. *Never Buy a Raccoon at a Gas Station* is her first book.